Pirouetting Hippos

Visions in Verse

GILL ROWE

Line drawings by
Jennifer Taggart

POTAMA HOUSE LIMITED

FOR CLIVE

Acknowledgements

With grateful thanks to Clive for his design input, Tom Stacey for reading the manuscript, Jenny Taggart for her inspired drawings, Robin Nott for his support, Malcolm and Alison Gordon for their invaluable research, Jane Havell for producing the book and to all my family and the many friends who encouraged me to publish.

CONTENTS

TRAVELLERS' TALES

ARRIVEDERCI

By Way of Introduction

When I was young I used to read about a noble pig.
His character was generous and his measurements were big.
Rejoicing in the title 'Count', his name was Curly Wee.
I'm still grateful for the legacy that he bequeathed to me.

For the exploits of this gallant pig were all set out in verse.
Than which, though only doggerel, you could do a whole
    lot worse.
Now whenever I've a pencil, paper and some time to spare
I can conjure up some verses, as by now you are aware.

For me it is impossible to be cast down for long.
For with metre, rhyme and scansion I've foundations for
    a song.
Yes, cadence, tone and rhythm, as many more have found,
Form the basis of the music that makes the world go round.

FIRST PERSON SINGULAR

Fitness First

I'm on my bike and pedalling,
I've had a thirty-minute swim.
Now I'm off to do some lunges,
All to keep up with *him*.

It's hard having a boyfriend
Who is such a fitness freak.
But at least I reap the benefit
Of his quite extraordinary physique!

The Gap Year

I'm going on my Gap Year.
I've earned time that's just for me.
I've waited long enough for it.
I'm nearly eighty-three!

I told my six grandchildren
I was going on a spree.
They all said, 'Good for Granny!'
One asked to accompany me.

But I don't want any baggage.
That would clip my new-spread wings.
I'm off to see the big wide world
And taste whatever fun it brings.

Did you hear about my Granny?
She went 'gapping' on her own.
We didn't hear a squeak for months.
She took no mobile phone.

But now she's sent a message
For circulation to us all:
'I'm staying here in Bali with
My toy-boy. Life's a ball!'

Mission Aborted

My hair is streaked, my eyebrows plucked,
My legs waxed and spray-tanned.
I've spent a bomb on products
From the latest make-up brand.
That should be all I need to catch
A gullible young man
With hormones, time and cash to spare.
(For that's mes vacances plan).

～

Oh *what* a waste of effort!
I'm calling it a day.
What is the point in staying here
When all the men are gay?

Wedding Plans

I'm going to get married, not in church, in a hotel.
For now, thank God, they've changed the rules it all works
    really well.
Your guests aren't inconvenienced by changes of venue.
You don't have to sing those boring hymns which I can't
    stand, can you?

The thing that's so much better about weddings which are mod
Is that now it's quite forbidden to even mention 'God'.
Though there's one teeny detail missing, and here I do not joke,
I've always thought a dog-collar's dead sexy on a bloke!

Tom and I have lived together so I know his little ways.
He wasn't keen at first, 'til I explained that weddings are
    the craze.
We've signed a *huge* agreement before we tie the knot
So if we split thereafter we know which of us gets what.

I've got my pure white bridal gown, with strapless fitted top.
The bridesmaids fancied trousers, but I soon gave that the chop!
The men are wearing morning suits with matching striped
    cravats.
The ladies will be all glammed up, and most of them in hats.

I'm going to have a string quartet, which lends a bit of style,
By way of compensation for not prancing down the aisle.
They're going to play my favourite tune, 'Forever and a Day',
Precisely at the moment when I plan to go away.

The day's arrived. The cake is made. It's almost time to dress.
What's this? A note from Tom: 'I'm sorry for this mess,
I've scarpered to Tunisia; under hugest stress.'
God, how *could* you do this? There's no forwarding address!

Grande Dame

I'll have Salade Niçoise with no tuna,
Poulet Provençale with no oil.
I like cheese, but no goat
And no garlic, please note.
(There's no end to the food I can spoil.)

What's the point of paying a fortune
To come to a five-star hotel
Unless you are the boss?
If you leave, it's their loss
So you've carte blanche for giving them hell!

Look at Me!

I'm this year's fashion 'must have'.
You'll see me here and there
For though 'exclusive' and 'designer'
I am taken everywhere.

They choose co-ordinating colours
For every smart event.
You'll have seen me in the photos
Wherever glitzy celebs went.

I've been close up to a royal.
I've seen endless movie stars.
To my owner I'd stay loyal
If she took me off to Mars!

I'm worn thrown across one shoulder
Or balanced on a hip.
I expect when I am older
I won't be taken on *each* trip.

For I know that when I'm bigger
I'll become more of a bore.
Now, as 'designer baby',
I know *just* what I'm here for.

Keeping Up Appearances

I look in the mirror and what do I see?
A fearsome old bag, but I recognise me.
Just hang on a minute, I'll put on my face.
After which, you'll admit, I'm no more a disgrace.

Now my cheeks glow with colour, my eyes have outline.
My lips glisten with gloss and my nose doesn't shine.
I'm fixing my hair using spray and some foam.
Then I'll tease and backcomb till it's shaped like the Dome.

I can't fathom these women, some quite half my age,
Who don't make an effort. They'll learn at some stage
That appearance is all; you *must* make a show.
But it doesn't come cheap, as I very well know.

There! I'm finished and looking, as usual, glam.
No one would know the whole thing is a sham.
I've persuaded myself that this person is me.
So tomorrow, who knows, when I look, what I'll see!

Escape Route

Me Mum has loads of fellas.
I never knew me Dad.
Me lovely Nan, she died last year.
No wonder I feel sad.

I haven't got a buddy
Though the crowd I'm with's not bad.
We bunk off school and hang around.
The boredom drives me mad.

I quite liked the old teacher,
He took an interest, see?
No one else, except for Nan,
Has ever valued me.

That Leroy, he's quite scary.
He knows a thing or two.
We done some cars, we done some dope.
There's nothing good to do.

I've had a load of cautions.
I was down the court last week.
A social worker came to call.
Me Mum said, 'What a cheek!'

They've given me a mentor.
We'll see what happens now.
At least she's fit, and not a bit
Like that other stupid cow.

I can't believe I've done it!
I've earned myself some cash.
The boss, who seems an okay bloke,
Drives a car that's really flash.

I've got on a mechanics' course.
I work with cars all day.
I'm with a really brilliant crowd.
I'm sorted, come what may.

LONDON LIVING

Interior Design

I'm paying for perfection in my latest London home.
The bathroom suite's from Germany, the marble from near
    Rome.
I've use the palest maple for the entertaining floors.
My designer did dear Lulu's yacht (the one based in the
    Azores).

It's been a total nightmare. I can't tell you the distress.
I've spent a bomb on massages and yoga for the stress.
But since we've had those darling Poles who are so good,
    and cheap,
We're getting there at last. Oh! Did you hear that little
    bleep?

That'll be François, my designer, now. He has a special ring.
I can talk to him at any time about almost anything.
He and I are quite a team. 'François? You're out of town?
What is that you're saying?' The house has been burned
    down.

Going to the Gym

It's half-past ten in Church Street
And I'm going to the gym.
I've got my Walkman and my shades.
I'm tall, I'm blonde, I'm slim.

It helps to have a figure
That's already lean of limb.
But you've got to make an effort
If you want to keep it trim.

I can't say I enjoy the weights.
They're most unfeminine.
But I quite fancy how I look
Fit, tanned and pencil-thin.

And while I do my lunges,
Pretending not to care,
I can eye up all the talent
And assess the likely fare.

You never know who you might meet
In work-outs at the gym.
And there's nothing like the latest gear
To show a well-toned limb.

I *always* make an effort
When I choose the clothes I wear
Though it looks as though they're just thrown on
Without the slightest care.

Today it's wide-flared hipsters,
Diamanté peep-toe shoes,
And a loose-knit top worn poncho-style
(The latest fashion news)

Round one more bend and here I am
As if upon a whim!
Omigod! What shall I do?
They've closed the bloody gym!

The Invitation

I've ringed round the date in my diary.
It is quite my favourite Oneth.
It's free for the mo, but as we all know
June's a really impossible month
What with Ascot and tennis and Henley
And Glyndebourne and parties and all.
I've a date for the Twoth, I can't change it in truth
For some Royals will be at that ball.
What's this name pencilled in? I can't read it.
Oh, of course, that relates to the Threeth.
It can change if I find something better.
It's only dinner with darling old Keith.
The Fourth next; that's always a fixture
(Well, actually, that isn't so.
It's only the name that remains just the same
But no matter) to Eton I go.
I could go through the month if you'd like
But quite frankly it's rather a bore.
Just hang on a mo. Remind me. Don't go.
Again, what was that nice invite *for*?

Going Places

I'm going to the RFH to hear the LMP
Last night it was the QEH, the band the OAE.
Don't think this is a BOGOF (that is 'Buy one, get one free')
I am the guest of my friend George de Trop, QC, MP.

Why Can't the English?

London's cosmopolitan, that's for certain sure.
I am sitting on a bus, the good old 94,
And about the only person, as far as I can see,
For whom English is their first, and native, language. Can this be?

There's Russian and Italian, also Spanish, French and Greek.
I recognise some Dutch, a language I for one don't speak!
Most people, it is true, are speaking English on this bus.
But in a range of accents which make it difficult to suss.

I realise, to my shame, that among the utterances let fall
There *is* English spoken by some natives after all.
These ugly sounds, which count for words (limited, in modern
    style)
Come from the young couple sitting right across the aisle.

He's tall, unshaven, scruffy, with baggy trousers and scuffed shoes.
She's young, blonde, semi-naked (with not a lot to lose).
I can't help hearing the exchange which is currently in flow:
'Oh shit, I've dropped me mobile!' 'Shift your arse. We gotta go.'

Recently, I'm sure I read, money was to be spent
On teaching English young to speak clearly, with intent.
They were going to have to listen to recordings of themselves
(I've long thought TEFL teaching aids should be on staff-room
    shelves).

But before assuming Higgins' role on such a monumental scale
A chilly word of warning, enough to turn taxpayers pale:
These unappealing youngsters, flouting elocution rules,
Are clearly both the products of expensive private schools!

Women's Liberation

What price emancipation?
It's the middle of the night
But I'm still at my office desk,
With not a soul in sight.

I leave for work each morning
In my smart black trouser suit.
Scooping up laptop, bag and phone,
Grabbing a piece of fruit.

I don't notice passing strangers
While rushing for my train.
I'm making calculations.
I have spreadsheets on the brain.

Is this what our sisters wanted
When they started up the fight
For women's liberation?
For me freedom's not in sight.

I'm locked into a lifestyle
That's a manic steeplechase.
I'm stressed out, tired and harassed.
You can see it in my face.

I've earned myself a fortune,
But whatever is the point
Of having loads of money
When your life is out of joint?

I know I am 'successful',
But I long to find a mate.
I'm going to quit this treadmill
Before it's all too late.

Fashion Guru

The halter-neck's from Hennes,
The shorts the latest style from Gap,
The bikini comes from M & S,
D'you wonder they go 'snap'?

The shops you find in every High Street
Serve their purpose very well.
But if you're aiming at distinctive chic
They have none of it to sell.

How much 'cooler' to be different
With clothes like no one else's kit.
Be a retro, suave sophisticate
Like me, and learn to knit!

Chalk and Cheese

'Lawks!
Them 'awks
'Is 'overing.
That's nature in the raw.
I'm
Going
Back to London.
I've 'ad enough of toof and claw.'

'This
City's
Terrifying.
The sirens and the crowds!
I'm
Going
Back to Scotland
To mountains, sea and clouds.'

Two,
Both true,
Opinions
Showing, if poles apart,
You'll
Never
Reach consensus
Without a change of heart.

Spoilt for Choice

Capuccino, espresso, macchiato and latte.
There's no end to the things you can choose.
Tai Chi, yoga, aerobics, massages, Pilates,
Try them all. You have nothing to lose.

Is that sun-dried or sun-blushed? House dressing or oil?
Would you like that with butter or soy?
In this make-believe world you must do as you choose.
You're admonished all day to 'Enjoy'.

How different things are on the Isla del Pascua.
Here you eat what there is, and rejoice.
There's no shopping to fit in, no cafés to sit in.
But contentment, unburdened by choice.

ANIMAL ANECDOTES

Ballerina Blues

I'm quite convinced that I'm a dancer. I'm certain in my
    mind.
I always stand with feet turned out, in third position you
    will find.
Every day I do my pliés and pas de chats of every kind.
You may say I haven't *quite* the shape. That's true. I am
    not blind.

My obsession with the ballet dates from when? This rings
    a bell.
Ever since I saw a quite delightful version of *Giselle*.
It was the grace and lightness of the steps for which I fell
And the twinkling of the pretty feet which danced so very
    well.

Oh, I forgot to mention that of these *I've* a second pair.
I've crossed them for the moment to get comfortable – there!
Now, where was I? Yes. *Giselle*. You'll not guess within a year
Where I saw it! At the circus. Yes. Right here.

    By the way, my name is Tama. I'm a Hippo.
    I'm getting some arthritis in my joints.
    Which is the *only* reason why, however hard you try,
    You'll not see me pirouetting on my points!

Max the Dachs

My name is Max.
A Wire-haired Dachs,
The recherché miniature version as you see.
But though I'm small
And cute and all
You'd be foolish if you tried to mess with me.

My pets are cool.
Good, as a rule.
Which is more than can be said about my food.
Yes, here's my lunch.
The biscuits crunch.
But that is all that I can say that isn't rude.

They've been to class.
Some silly ass
Told them not to give me luscious meat and all.
So there it is.
It's all there is.
This boring formula stuff does not enthral.

I dig outside.
The garden's wide
And you never know what treasures you may find.
I get up roots,
I eat young shoots.
Well, I need something to get menus off my mind!

I have a plan
To make them ban
That insulting tasteless veterinary dross.
I'll eat their plants.
My giddy aunts!
Then they'll soon know that I'm the boss!

Lion Wisdom

These cubs will be the death of me.
They're cheeky and they're bold.
I have to keep reminding them
'Respect those who are old.'

I can't think why those human things
Have stopped doing the same.
The way their young talk back at them –
Well, it's a crying shame.

It fair would take your breath away
Things I've heard when they are near.
That's why I take my cubs away.
I don't want them to hear!

Game Park Gossip

I've got an itch which I can't reach.
Scratch if for me, there's a love.
Jeeps! What's that appalling racket
From the neighbours up above?

Honestly, it's *so* difficult
To get a moment's peace.
Oh, by the way. I need your help
I'm worried about my niece.

She's so hopeless with her daughters.
It makes me very sad.
When she does try to rein them in
They go running to their Dad.

The boy is worse. He's joined a gang.
He's unruly and uncouth.
Though sometimes he just larks about
Like any other baboon youth.

Oh, look! A band of human beans
Has stopped to watch us play.
That one in front's the double
Of my dear old Auntie May!

Elephant Cake-walk

Swinging slowly down towards us
Ears flapping, elephants appear.
These noble, massive beasts, we're told,
Should not give rise to fear.

You're not in any danger
Unless they're thwarted in some way.
But if 'in musk' they point a tusk
I'd get the hell away!

A la Côte d'Azur

I've got my special toiletries
In a handsome tartan grip.
There's shampoo and conditioner,
Prescription ointment for my lip.

In the secret inner pocket
You'll find an extra little treat.
For you never can be sure, abroad,
Just what is safe to eat.

This year I've got a snazzy
New designer piece of kit.
It's a scarf with matching visor cap.
A really perfect fit.

The only problem I envisage
On hol à la Côte d'Azur,
Is the really quite excessive heat
Which for me has no allure.

Oh, by the way, I never said.
Just so you know the score.
I'm quite the most enchanting
Pekinese you ever saw!

The Swallow

Just consider for a moment the genius of the swallow.
One announces when it's time to go and all the rest will
    follow.
They swoop, they chat, they spread the word. This is their
    preparation.
They need no bags or tickets for their annual peregrination.
What a contrast to ourselves when we start planning long-
    haul travel.
So many clothes and papers and instructions to unravel!
The piles of 'quite essential' kit we carry when we roam
From medicines to toiletries, clothes, shoes, bags, mobile
    phone.
How come we need this baggage, we who are so very wise
When tiny little swallows fly the world with no supplies?

The Seagull

The seagull's got a problem.
It's limping as it walks.
It's on its own. The rest don't seem
To hear its plaintive squawks.

But suddenly it brightens.
It skips and comes to life!
For why? Of course! He's summoned,
And she's here, his loving wife.

The Giraffe

Gentle of eye
With air serene
And calm, unhurried gait,
This elegant
Young ruminant
Observes me as we wait.

Her dappled coat
And fine long throat,
Half-hidden by the trees,
Reminds us that,
Unlike the cat,
Her staple diet is leaves.

In the quiet air
We hear her tear
At branches high above.
Of all wild creatures
This one's features
Inspire my greatest love.

I Know My Place

Elephant, lion, impala, giraffe,
Zebra, hippo, klip-springer and snake.
Crocodile, rhino, fish eagle, baboon.
Size, shape, colour determined by 'make'.

Kruger Park lifestyle, its rhythm, its pace
Follows patterns determined by beast.
Foraging, feeding, asleep or at play
They're the stars. For once man matters least.

Animals, like those observed in the wild,
Know their place in the order of things.
Grandma's a grandma, a child is a child,
And not one would expect to sprout wings.

Should we not learn from observing this scene
That it's not always wise to be 'driven'.
Recognise limits and be as you are.
Just be happy with what you've been given.

HEALTH 'ISSUES'

The Clinic

Sitting in the clinic, after very short a while
You'll note the inefficient, wasteful, antiquated style.
Despite the good intentions and the kindness of the staff
The whole place is a shambles. It's enough to make you
    laugh.

I'd been sent to have a blood test at least two days before
On the grounds of saving time. But still I have a whole
    lot more.
Then I sit and wait for ages to be measured, after which
I'm moved two places 'up'. For why? My nerves begin to
    twitch.

And while I sit and wonder what on earth it's all about
A young girl with a clip-board keeps tripping in and out.
I spy a slim young doctor, not much older than my son,
And I venture, 'Where's the specialist?' Well, today this
    lad's the one.

He hadn't got a clue about my history, or the test
That I came to have two days ago, though I'm sure he
    did his best.
Needless to say my confidence by now had sunk to nil.
By the time I left the clinic I felt seriously ill!

Sugar-Free

You're counting carbs? Try sugar-free.
Good-oh, I thought, that's just for me,
Until I read the small print
Which left me all at sea.

I start off with Nutrition Facts.
The first one that I see
Is 'serving size three cookies'.
If that's a 'fact' I'm Tweedledee.

What with sodium stearoyl lactylate
And Xanthum gum (cave!)
Also thiamine mononitrate,
It's double Dutch to me.

They've coined a whole new language
Which should be clear as ABC.
But to make any sense of it
You need at least a PhD.

Take the label on this packet
Which states, explicitly
'Sugar 0 grammes' (zero, to me)
'Sugar alcohol 6g!'

Or take 'exchange information'
By way of an e.g.
Does this bear some relation
To financial currency?

No. 'Exchange lists' deal in fats
And carbs, measured *so* carefully.
But how and why they operate
Is clothed in mystery.

There's a simple explanation
For this guff let's all recall.
It's to make us fail to notice
We're not eating food at all!

Manuka Therapy

The leaves of the Manuka
Have healing qualities unique.
They can vanquish a verruca
Or revive a tired physique.

Cook's ally against scurvy.
Friend to insomniac.
Best of all, if things go pear-shaped,
It's an aphrodisiac!

Gout

My husband's got gout.
You'd better watch out!
I'd keep on the right side of him.
He'll hobble about
But will give you a clout
If you get near his agonised limb.

He's mild, as a rule,
And demonstrably cool.
He's considerate, charming and kind.
But when he's got gout
His demon will out.
Then a crankier gent you won't find!

His fuse becomes short.
All help counts for nought.
His furious one-liners cut ice.
But once the damned gout
Is over and out
He's restored to himself in a trice.

'Beauty Sencials'

'Beauty sencials'. What are they?
I'm at a loss to know.
One girl's just come out of there
With nothing much to show.

Are they machines or treatments?
What are 'sencials' for?
Spare parts, perhaps, for servicings.
Or worse – a full rebore.

Should you ever meet a 'sencial'
Do tell me what you see.
If you find it makes you gorgeous
Please acquire one, just for me!

The Reluctant Counsellor

Don't tell me your story
I don't want to know.
Let's leave it a mystery.
Okay?

You've told me your ailments
In tedious detail.
Emotional derailments?
No way!

This garrulous stranger
Unburdening his soul
Will run into danger
One day.

Perhaps I should lend him
Some warning device
So that others can send him
Away.

But hang on a moment!
Is it too much to ask?
Forgive my impatience
I pray.

He may have no friend to
Offload all his 'stuff'
As the rest of us tend to
Each day.

And if talking (no vice)
Can restore this man's soul,
Listening's surely a small price
To pay.

Feeling 'Off'

I'm feeling 'off',
I've got a cough.
There's a pain in my left side.
I'm out of sorts.
Can't summon thoughts
To stem this gloomy tide.

What's this? A light
Of dazzling white
Has flashed before my eyes.
Across my glance
The colours dance.
Released, my spirit flies.

I see once more
The rocky shore.
The wondrous land, sea, sky.
My ailments flee.
Of them I'm free.
Who can say how or why?

The Pessimist and the Optimist

It's hard being a pessimist.
People won't let you be.
They'll always try and cheer you up.
It's dreadful to be me.

If you say the weather's muck,
Which any fool can see,
Some spark will say, 'It's brightening!'
Why can't they just agree?

It's such fun being an optimist.
I know that life's a ball.
To cheer up some poor misery
Is the greatest joy of all!

Pointless Comparisons

Each one of us is different, so it's very plain to see
That comparisons are pointless, for there's always sure to be
Someone who is bigger, smaller, older, younger,
Heavier, lighter, fatter, thinner, more or less intelligent
    than me.

Take young Kylie from The Gables, who is huge compared
    to Dwee,
But put her next to dear old Pru, she shrinks considerably.
Likewise Eldyne from the bookshop. Well, any fool can see
That she's cleverer far than Jane but a thicko next to Fi!

Why make all these comparisons? Just think. What is the
    point?
You might find that such comparing puts your nose right
    out of joint!
For it remains a scientific fact that no matter what you do
There'll be someone, somewhere, richer, happier and more
    talented than you.

But this doesn't make them better than their neighbours,
    don't you see?
It's just that we're all different. That's how it's meant to be.
So away with all comparisons. Be happy just to see
And enjoy, in all its spiciness, life's great variety.

HANDLE WITH CARE

Fair Nefertiti

My name's Nefertiti.
I come from Tahiti.
You think I'm a sweetie.
You're wrong.

I dress oh so neatly
(A tad incompletely)
In either grass skirt or
Sarong.

You may gaze with entreaty
At fair Nefertiti
Whose thighs are so meaty
And strong.

But once try to treaty
Or make her your sweetie
She'll finish you off with
Her thong!

On the Mobile

Mobile clamped to her left ear, back hunched against the rain,
She lugs her heavy photo gear, face screwed up, as if in pain.
'I can't believe you said that. You're talking utter crap.
Of course I can't. Don't ask again.' The lid shut with a snap.

What now? I thought. And who's the guy who got it in
    the neck?
She squared her shoulders, tossed her hair, resumed her furious
    trek.
The angry clicking of her heels recedes. That scene's complete.
A blessed calm descends upon the peaceful tree-lined street.

Telephone Tantrum

I don't *want* to press a button
I don't *want* a stupid choice
I don't fit any 'option'
I want a human voice.

I *hate* my touch-tone telephone
I *hate* being put on 'hold'
I'm boiling in the danger zone
And ready to explode.

I *detest* the tinny music
That's supposed to calm my nerves
I *loathe* being left in limbo
I want a 'him wot serves'!

I want to hear a person
Who understands my plight
Not an automated help line
Based in the Isle of Wight!

At last! I'm through! A real live voice!
I take back all I said.
What's this? I don't *believe* it!
The bloody line's gone dead!

Provocation

Adorned with flowers, birds, butterfly,
Her blue jeans hug her shapely thigh.
While further north tanned, bare and lean
A midriff beautifies the scene.
Her glance takes in, with some disdain,
Those passengers waiting for her plane.
It's 'cool' so young this pose to acquire.
If she but knew. She plays with fire.

Loose Cannon!

'Suit yourself, you idiot.
Don't blame me if you get burned.
Why should I care about your skin
When you have never learned?

I brought you down a T-shirt
But all you do is give me grief!'
This tirade, in fluent Italian,
Resounds across the reef.

Her voice pitched high with anger,
Frustration and abuse,
Radios to all a warning:
There's a cannon on the loose!

Not Singing in the Rain

I knew it! I said it would rain.
This is serious. Don't mention a drain.
I got myself pretty
To go out in the city.
I spent hours and it's all been in vain.

For I cannot go out in the rain.
My persona'd be ruined, that's plain
With face and hair battered
And stockings all spattered.
I'm frustrated all over again.

I'm a tolerant soul, in the main.
I'll put up, as you know, with great pain.
But if I am thwarted
Or my plans are aborted
Watch out, for I'll really complain.

Salaam Madame

With pouting lips
And swaying hips,
Heavy jewellery in gold,
Her look commands.
Her voice demands
Although she's not that old.

How's she contrived,
Controlled, connived
To have things all her way?
She cuts up rough
When things get tough:
'Or else . . . I'll go away.'

Some little boys
They lost their toys
When Mummy went away.
So ever more
They will ensure
Their womenfolk don't stray.

This means, I fear,
The cost is dear.
They'll humour them *all* the way.
So you'll see 'Salaams'
To spoiled Mesdames
Wherever you may stray.

Tough Cookie

My hair is short.
My tone is sharp.
I register discontent.
I never pause
To wonder where
My femininity went.

REFLECTIONS FROM THE CONTINENT

The Beautiful Couple

I love the turquoise glasses
From St Tropez, I declare.
The matching streaks of colour
In the stylish ash-blonde hair.
The diaphanous turquoise wrap
Held together with a pin. The same
Sparkle on the high-heeled mules
(These very tall and thin).

She has taken so much trouble
Every bit has been worthwhile.
She's a very pretty girl
With a lovely open smile.
Her companion, who adores her,
Is an attractive boy.
Thank you, to the pair of you.
To behold you is a joy!

Transposition

It's odd to see one's neighbours
Semi-naked à la plage.
Especially since most of us
Are of un certain âge!

I picture us in Knightsbridge
Only scantily attired.
The prospect's inconceivable
But my imagination's fired!

I can see old Mrs Whatsit
With her double chin and tum
Parading right down Sloane Street
Her not inconsiderable bum.

As for Mr Whodyoumeflip
With his wispy hairy chest
And his bandy little leglets
Why, he too has left the nest!

I see him in my mind's eye
Garbed in those diminutive blue trunks
Not fazed one jot or tittle
By passing Antipodean hunks.

Of course this is all nonsense.
England is far too cold.
Just don't imagine we're inhibited
Because we're getting old!

Three's a Crowd

Extended on my lounger, I am trying to ignore
The poignant little drama that is playing out next door
Involving mother, teenage daughter and mother's paramour.
I'd encountered this young lady on the stairs some time before.
Her truculent expression promised trouble heaped in store.
I'd just assumed this was because, at that age, life's a bore.

But it is so much worse than this for everyone has rowed.
The mother, tall and arrogant; the lover, also proud.
The little girl (for so she is) inside so hurt and cowed
Exudes ingratitude for things with which she's been endowed.
How else can she express her pain? 'This shouldn't be allowed.'
Ah me! For here, it's plain to see, three really is a crowd.

Mademoiselle

She trips along the terrace
With a jaunty, carefree air,
Studiously indifferent
To all who stop and stare.

Her trim form is enveloped
In a wrap of startling pink.
Her hair piled up upon her head
With more care than you'd think.

She's wearing thick-soled flip-flops,
Her nails are painted rose.
Affecting disapproval,
She has wrinkled up her nose.

She accepts admiring glances
As if they were her due.
Yesterday she was attired
In various shades of blue.

She has modelled her appearance
On the one who passed before.
No compliments will faze her.
She has heard them all before!

It is safe to make predictions
Of the one she is to be.
Her mother said some time ago
'The angel's just like me!'

I shiver in my swimsuit
When I think of what's in store.
For this model of perfection
Is as yet no more than four!

Summer Musings

I soak up smells and sounds of summer as heat penetrates
　　my bones.
Sun-tan lotion, chink of glasses, ever-present mobile phones.
Languid conversations under cheery parasols.
All the familiar attributes of lazy summer hols.

A tiny little lizard has materialised, I see.
It's hanging on and breathing hard and blinking up at me.
I picture it returning home, exhausted, to its mate
With no end of curious stories and adventures to relate.

'You'll never guess what happened when at the beach today!'
What's exciting for a lizard I find very hard to say.
But I imagine that, in essence, it is very much the same
For every one of God's created, no matter what the name.

We were all born with our instincts for survival and the rest.
We need to eat, we need to sleep to keep our accustomed zest.
So next time you think of swatting a mosquito or a flea
Reflect again a moment, for it could be you or me!

The Diplomatic Wife

She's a very tiresome woman.
A fearsome, raging snob.
Her husband was a diplomat.
Now that's a *proper* job.
She's always dropping names
As from a monumental height.
Most of whom, in truth, don't ever
Know her, even by sight.

She shoots the most fantastic line,
If given half a chance,
About former foreign postings.
Her darting little glance
Is constantly in action
(Which gives the game away)
Monitoring your reaction
To what she has to say.

How it matters that she's 'someone'.
What a shame that she must be
Always trying to make up
For some perceived deficiency.
For she has some real talents
And her heart's in the right place.
Beneath the careful make-up
There was once a pretty face.

I feel sorry for her husband
Who's a really decent sort,
And bright! It's sad he never went
As far as people thought he ought.
No, he never reached high echelons
Of diplomatic life.
And the reason? Well you've guessed it.
His quite appalling wife!

Fond Farewell

'Ma chère Madame. Je suis desolée. Vous partez à midi.'
'Mais oui,' I smile. For hid within this French hyperbole
There lies another meaning which is plain for all to see:
Thank God they're off! The coast is clear. So all the more
　　for me!

TRAVELLERS' TALES

Sweet Revenge

Thwack! A monumental back-pack attacks me on the head.
What is it that these travellers pack that so resembles lead?
Squish! A gross Italian rump has landed on my thigh.
Its owner hasn't noticed (or not stopped to question why).
A German wearing hiking boots has stamped upon my toe.
To hell with this. I've had enough. This time *I'll* have a go!

The Tour Boat

The landscape's majestic
The views are sublime.
Shame we creatures domestic
Don't go in for mime.

The racket they're making's
Attacking my head.
After hours in this Bedlam
You'd rather be dead.

Behind me two women
Screech into my ear.
Then they scream at their husbands
Two rows to the rear.

Now the guide's banging on
His tones strident, yet blurred,
In five different lingos.
His endeavour's absurd.

The boat engine's throbbing.
You can't hear a word
So everyone's yelling
To make themselves heard.

Around me some Brits
Exchange looks of despair.
Once the deck doors are open
We flee to fresh air.

The relief of the quiet
As all tension it shelves.
Now at last nature's wonders
Can speak for themselves.

Travelling Companions

They're travelling together, two couples from L.A.
But why they chose to come here I shouldn't care to say.
The silver sand? The waving palms? The snorkelling on
    the reef?
No. They sit playing bridge all day, giving each other grief!

Business Class

Travel in Business, you'll find yourself charmed.
All objections to flying are swiftly disarmed.
You'll be welcomed aboard, you'll be offered champagne,
It's spacious and restful, not a bit like a plane.
There's a present, of toothbrush and lip-salve and socks
Packed neatly away in a dear little box.
When you're settled and airborne they offer more booze.
There are pillows and blankets, but put off your snooze
'Til you've mastered the gadgets. You're in for a treat.
At a touch change the angle of footrest and seat,
Then extract from the armrest your own special screen
To view movies the like of which you've never seen!
They'll come round with cocktails and water and wine
And menus so tempting they're hard to decline.
It'll cost you a fortune. But it's surely worthwhile
If for once in your life you have travelled in style!

Tahiti Airport

The Gallic shrug
Says Je m'en fou!
I couldn't give a toss.
Find out yourself
Where you should go.
Don't bother me. I'm cross.

I'm hot. I'm bored.
I hate my job.
My boyfriend's buggered off.
All right for you
In Business Class.
You're treated like a toff.

I'll make you pay.
Unpack your bags.
Let's see what you have got.
Oh, what the hell!
I couldn't care.
You'd better keep the lot.

The International Date Line

The date's been ate!
It's gobbled up.
It's vanished from our lives.
What curious
Deprivations
This travelling contrives.

We decided
To go backwards
i.e. to travel west
So we always had
Some time in hand,
Which must be for the best.

But suddenly
It's different.
We've crossed the line to find
Without ever
Even seeing it
We've left a whole day behind!

New Horizons

The massive mountain ranges
Of this amazing land
Now resemble crumpled tissue
Paper, below on either hand.

Those same peaks that left us speechless
By their grandeur and their scale
Now, like fingered pastry cases,
Appear fragile, delicate and pale.

Life is shaped by how we see things.
So if you have a point of view
Always be prepared to change it
And you'll see the world anew.

In a Hobart Garden

Anenomes, roses, delphiniums and jasmine
All bloom on this island, discovered by Tasman.
Wisteria's entwined in the iron balustrade
Fringing the balcony's welcoming shade.

This garden so fragrant, so English in style!
You could blink and be back there if just for a while.
Which all goes to show that wherever we roam
We carry within us an echo of home.

Don't be a Tosser

Don't be a tosser. Bin your butts.
(Aussie for No Litter Please).
It took *me* a while to decipher.
Just pity the poor Japanese!

Coral Island

The wheeling seagulls squabble as they circle overhead
While unperturbed, beneath them, a turtle lifts its head
Out of crystal, turquoise water on its way across the bay.
This, on tranquil Coral Island, is just a normal day.
Lizards snuff and forage. Butterflies of vivid hue
Flutter round tumbling orange flowers, while a snow-white
     cockatoo
Soars up into the azure sky on business of its own.
This place is quite idyllic *and* – there's not one single
     mobile phone!

Revelation

The air is stale. The food is dire.
I'm squeezed into my seat.
That baby's yelled for half an hour.
The tedium is complete.

Turning my head to ease my neck
Through the window I behold
An astonishing array of hues –
Blue, orange, burnished gold.

Awestruck, I watch the sunset fade
To discover, in a trice,
My selfish grumblings silenced
By this glimpse of paradise.

ARRIVEDERCI

Dropping a Perpendicular

Bang goes a perpendicular!
I dropped it. Can't think why.
What is the use of this straight line
Stretching earthwards from the sky?

I know. I'll slither down it.
Then, stretching out my feet.
I'll sit (at the right angle)
And plan another treat.

First published in 2005 by
Potama House Limited
P. O. Box 50427
London W8 9AF
www.potamahouse.co.uk

© 2005 Gill Rowe

Line drawings by Jennifer Taggart
Cover © Potama House Limited
Produced by Jane Havell Associates
Printed by Thanet Press

ISBN 0 9551038 0 0